VICTORIAN BRITAIN

JANE SHUTER

H www.heinemann.co.uk
Visit our website to find out more information about Heinemann books.

To order:
☎ Phone 44 (0) 1865 888020
▤ Send a fax to 44 (0) 1865 314091
▢ Visit the Heinemann Bookshop at www.heinemann.co.uk to browse our catalogue and order online.

First published in Great Britain by Heinemann Library, Halley Court, Jordan Hill, Oxford OX2 8EJ, a division of Reed Educational and Professional Publishing Ltd. Heinemann is a registered trademark of Reed Educational & Professional Publishing Ltd.

OXFORD MELBOURNE AUCKLAND JOHANNESBURG BLANTYRE
GABORONE IBADAN PORTSMOUTH (NH) USA CHICAGO

Designed by Celia Floyd
Illustrations by Jeff Edwards
Originated by Dot Gradations
Printed in Hong Kong

05 04 03 02 01
10 9 8 7 6 5 4 3 2 1
ISBN 0 431 10204 X (hardback)

05 04 03 02
10 9 8 7 6 5 4 3
ISBN 0 431 10213 9 (paperback)

British Library Cataloguing in Publication Data

Shuter, Jane
  Victorian Britain. – (Exploring history)
  1. Great Britain – History – Victoria, 1837-1901
  2. Great Britain – Social conditions – 19th century
  I. Title
  941'.081

Acknowledgements

The Publishers would like to thank the following for permission to reproduce photographs:
Bridgeman Art Library: Pg.5, Pg.6, Pg.16, Pg.22; Edifice/Gillian Darley: Pg.26; Format/M Murray: Pg.18; Fotomas: Pg.10; Hulton: Pg.4, Pg.7, Pg.8, Pg.13, Pg.15, Pg.20; Mary Evans: Pg.12, Pg.27; REPP/Heinemann: Pg.17, Pg.19, Pg.21, Pg.25; Topham Picturepoint: Pg.14.

Cover photograph reproduced with permission of Fotomas Index.

Every effort has been made to contact copyright holders of any material reproduced in this book. Any omissions will be rectified in subsequent printings if notice is given to the Publisher.

Any words appearing in the text in bold, **like this**, are explained in the glossary.

Contents

What was it like for children living in Victorian Britain?

Who were the Victorians and when did they live?

When we talk about 'the Victorians', we mean people who lived in Britain during the **reign** of Queen Victoria (1837-1901). During Victoria's long reign Britain became an important world power. Victorian businessmen were able to use the steam-powered machines invented in the years before Victoria became queen to make Britain the first **industrialized** nation. Industry made Britain rich and being rich made Britain powerful.

Just because Britain was rich does not mean that everyone in the country was rich. There were far more people in Britain struggling to make a living than rich people, all through the period. Matters were made worse because, to begin with, the government did not believe it was their job to help to improve living and working conditions.

1840	1850	1860	1870	1880	1890	1900

1837 Queen Victoria comes to the throne	1851 Great Exhibition	1870 Dr Barnardo opens first home for boys	1880 Children must go to school from age 5-13	1901 Queen Victoria dies

Queen Victoria, Prince Albert and their children photographed at Osborne House, their home on the Isle of Wight, in 1857. Photography was invented in 1839.

These poor families, painted in 1874, have no homes. They are waiting to go into the **workhouse**, where they will be split up and given work.

Victorian children

In some ways, life was the same for all Victorian children. They were not seen as having 'rights' – they were being brought up by adults and had to learn from them. They were expected to do as they were told.

Victorian children had very different lives depending on whether they lived in the town or the country, how rich their parents were and what social class they came from. These things affected whether you had to work, where you lived, whether you got enough to eat – even whether you died young. In general, rich children had a sheltered life with comfortable homes. The poorer a child's family was the more likely they were to have to work from an early age and be badly housed and fed.

Queen Victoria (1819–1901)

Victoria was born in May 1819. She became queen in 1837, when she was only eighteen. She married Prince Albert in 1840 and had four sons and five daughters. Personal disaster changed Victoria's life, and the way she ruled the country, when Albert died of typhoid in 1861. Victoria mourned him deeply for the rest of her life. She stopped making public appearances and began to lose popularity. She ruled until 1901, longer than any other British monarch.

Exploring further

The Heinemann Explore CD-ROM will give you information about Victorian Britain. From the Contents screen you can click on the blue words to find out about the Victorians.

Class

Victorian society was divided up by a complicated class system depending mainly on how well off people were. The simplest class division was between upper class (the rich and powerful, who had no need to work), the **middle class** (the well-off who worked as bankers, doctors or ran their own businesses) and the **working class** (who did the hard, manual work on farms and in factories or who worked in shops and businesses owned by other people). However, each of these classes had many separate levels. A poor shopkeeper, who was at the bottom of the middle class, would have more in common with someone at the top of the working class than with a well-off, middle class doctor.

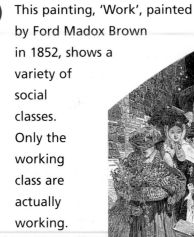

Worlds apart

Benjamin Disraeli, a politician, wrote a novel called *Sybil* in 1846, in which he discussed the huge difference between rich and poor at the time:

They are two nations who have no contact or sympathy, who know as little of each other's habits, thoughts and feelings as if they lived on different planets. They have been bred differently, fed on different food. They have different manners and obey different laws.

This painting, 'Work', painted by Ford Madox Brown in 1852, shows a variety of social classes. Only the working class are actually working.

Rich people often had their domestic servants photographed.

Servants: an example of class divisions

Servants were all working class. Yet if we look at the way just one group, indoor servants, were organized in a well-off middle class household in about 1860, we can see how complicated the class system was. The most important of the indoor servants was the butler, who organized all the other servants. He could earn about £50 a year. The cook was the most important of the kitchen staff. She could earn up to £30 a year. She had several servants to help her. The least important of these was the **scullery** maid. She would earn £9 a year at the most. While the butler and the scullery maid were both seen as working class by their employers, they certainly did not see themselves as being in the same social class.

Domestic service

Domestic service was one of the most common jobs for girls and women. Many girls took their first job close to home, but they often had to move around. They found work by reading newspaper adverts or going to regular '**hiring fairs**' in towns.

Exploring further – Victorian people

The CD-ROM contains information about all sorts of Victorian People, from Queen Victoria to Lucy Luck. Follow this path: Contents > Biographies

Click on the names in blue to find out about them.

Looking at life

Victorian Britain was a wealthy, powerful country. In 1851 the Great Exhibition was organized in Britain, to celebrate 'the industry of all nations'. The nation with the most exhibits, naturally, was Britain.

Britain was rich and powerful mostly because of money made through trade. British businessmen could give good prices for various **manufactured** goods, from cotton to iron rails, because Britain was the first nation to use steam power in **factories**. Goods could be mass-produced quickly and cheaply. At the beginning of the Victorian period this meant that British businesses made huge **profits**. By the end of the period, as other countries became **industrialized**, Britain was losing her trading advantage.

Factory towns

The new factories needed more people to work in them, so many towns grew rapidly. In 1801 the population of Leeds was 53,000. By 1851 it was 172,000 and by 1901 it was 429,000. The homes that were built for workers were built cheaply and were crammed full of working families. They seldom had drains or a fresh water supply, so became places where disease could start and spread quickly.

Crystal Palace, home of the Great Exhibition, was made from mass-produced metal and glass parts, brought to London by train and put together in Hyde Park.

By 1901 the British Empire had spread right across the globe. The Empire was connected by railway, steamship and telegraph cable. It was held together by the army.

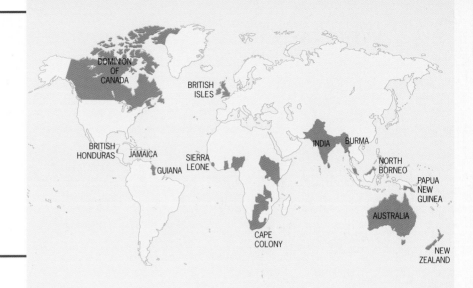

Building an Empire

The Victorians were sure that it was a good thing for Britain to take over and 'civilize' other countries. They thought British ways were best, so it would be good for any nation to be brought British religion, laws and ideas. This also meant that the British could make these countries buy British goods and sell their goods to Britain cheaply.

Self-help

Victorian Britain had a lot of poor people. In the 1830s the government was unwilling to pass laws about work, education or town planning to help the poor. Many people, including MPs, believed the government had no right to make laws about these things. They felt that if the government made laws to help people they would make these people even weaker and more in need of help. People believed in 'self-help'; doing something to make things better. As time went on the government came to see that there were some things that 'self-help' could not put right. They passed laws about work, public health, education and care for the poor.

Exploring further – The British Empire

Follow this path to discover more about the British Empire:

Contents > Exploring > Invasion and Warfare > The British Empire

What was life like for a poor child in the 1840s?

Poor people were at the bottom of the class system. They were **working class** people who were either earning just enough to survive or who were not earning even that. People with no money and no work had no way to support themselves and their families were called **paupers**. Various groups gave some help to paupers. There was no help at all for the struggling poor, who earned money but not enough to support themselves properly.

Out to work

Poor families needed everyone in the family working, from as young an age as possible. Often, especially in **factories**, children and women could find work more easily than men. As long as a job did not need physical strength, employers preferred to hire women and children since they could pay them lower wages.

Working at home

Many women and children took jobs working from home, making such things as matchboxes, cigars or brooms. This work was very badly paid. However, the mother and children could work together, so the children were looked after.

Even before Queen Victoria's **reign**, laws were passed to limit the age at which children worked in factories. But there were very few inspections, and factory owners often ignored these laws.

Working children

In 1851, the **census** showed there were just under 18,000,000 people living in England and Wales. About 6,372,000 of these people were aged 0-15. Below is a table of children's jobs surveyed in 1841 and in 1881. This survey found 972,600 children working in these jobs alone. This number does not include the hundreds of children working from homes, cleaning chimneys, sweeping the streets and doing other kinds of work not on the list.

Type of work	Date	
	1841	1881
Farming	216,400	70,300
Mining	47,900	26,200
Fuel, gas, chemicals	800	600
Wood-working	23,100	5000
Cloth and clothes-making	564,700	145,600
Working at docks	13,200	48,400
Railways	100	1800
Army or Navy	6900	500
Servants	99,500	105,100
Total working	972,600	403,500

Exploring further – Children at work

Writing from the time can help us to learn more about the terrible conditions endured by working children at the time that Victoria came to the throne. Follow this path: Contents > Written Sources > Tom the Chimneysweep

Factory work

In the 1840s the fastest growing industry was the cloth-making industry. **Factories** were built all over England, especially in the north-west. Cloth-making factories needed lots of workers. Factory owners preferred to employ children. They could pay children less. Also, children were small, so could crawl under the machines to mend broken threads.

By 1840 there had already been one law passed to limit the age at which children started working and the hours they worked. During the 1840s more laws were passed. However, many factory owners broke the rules. Children worked long hours in hot, dusty rooms. They had few breaks and the machinery was very dangerous. Injuries were common.

This man, talking to investigators in 1832, could not find work, nor could his wife. His children were the only workers in the family:

At the busy time of year, my wife and I get them up at 2 in the morning and they are seldom in bed before 11 at night. The rest of the time they work from 6 in the morning to half past 8 at night. They are so tired by this work that they fall asleep with their supper in their mouths. My eldest had her finger caught in a cog and screwed off below the knuckle.

Not all mills broke the law. In this mill there are men and women working, but not children.

Young children in coal mines worked hard for long hours in near darkness.

Mine work

In the 1840 many young children worked in the mines that produced the coal to drive steam-powered machines. The youngest of them did the easiest jobs, opening the '**traps**', or doors, for the coal carts. These 'trappers' were as young as six years old. Older, stronger, children pulled the carts. Boys went on to become miners as soon as they were strong enough. There were laws passed to control the work of children in mines. Mine owners, just like factory owners, often ignored the laws to make a bigger profit.

Other work

We know most about the work that children did in factories and mines, because the government investigated conditions and we can read the reports. But children worked in many other industries, such as brick making, pottery making and the building trade. They also worked for chimney sweeps, shopkeepers and as servants in private houses.

Exploring further – The workhouse

The poorest people had to live in the workhouse. Follow this path to discover more about these places:

Contents > Exploring > Everyday Life > Workhouses

Who helped to improve the lives of Victorian children?

During the Victorian period many people tried to improve the lives of poor children. Laws were passed to control working conditions and homeless children were found homes and work. Reporters, writers and MPs made people aware of the terrible conditions poor children lived in. Women from well-off families visited local poor families with food or old clothes. In some country districts this was all the help the poor got. Some people formed groups to help the poor. The help they gave varied, but included basic food, clothing and shelter. One of the most famous of these was the Salvation Army, set up by William Booth in 1865.

Doctor Barnardo

Thomas John Barnardo (1845–1905) was born in Dublin. In 1866 he moved to London to study at the missionary school. He preached and worked for the poor in the East End of London. In 1867 he set up the East End Juvenile **Mission** in Stepney. His aim was to provide poor, homeless children with food, shelter and training, so that they could support themselves. In 1870, he set up the first of his homes for boys. He also set up missions for the poor. By the time of his death the homes he set up had rescued and trained about 60,000 children.

Popular writers, like Charles Dickens, used their novels (this illustration is from *The Old Curiosity Shop*) to show the problems of poverty.

1833 Factory Act:	Starting age 9. Hours age 9-13 = 9; age 13-16 = 12; no night work for those under 18.
1842 Mines Act:	Starting age (underground) 10, for boys; no women or girls to work underground.
1844 Factory Act:	Hours age 9-13 = 6.5; age 13-18 = 12; dangerous machinery to be fenced in.
1847 Factory Act:	Hours age 9-18 = 10, night and day. This was raised to 10.5 hours in 1850.
1850 Mines Act:	Starting age (underground) 10; safety measures improved.
1860 Mines Act:	Starting age (underground) 12; safety measures improved.
1867 Factory Act:	All factory workers on a 10 hour day.

Changing the laws: Lord Shaftesbury and other MPs

From 1833 on through the Victorian period laws were passed that regulated children's work. The laws reduced the hours children could work and raised the age at which they could start work. Above are the most important laws for **factories** and mines and how they affected children.

The Earl of (Lord) Shaftesbury and other reformers visited mines and factories, to see conditions for themselves.

Exploring further – People who helped

To find more information about Dr Barnardo and Lord Shaftesbury, click on Search on the top panel of the Contents page. Pick the name you want to search for from the keywords on the next page and click on Enter. The screen will now show a list of pages on the CD-ROM that mention them. Click on the names of the pages to find out what they show.

What was it like going to school at the end of the nineteenth century?

Before looking at schools at the end of the nineteenth century, we need to look at how schools were organized at the beginning of the Victorian period, so we can see how things changed.

Schools in the 1840s

In the 1840s upper and **middle class** children went to school. Most poor children did not. Almost all education was paid for and people thought it was most important to educate boys. There were only a few girls' schools, which taught girls the skills they would need to run a home and mix with other people of their social class. Many boys were taught in 'boarding schools', living at the school in term time and only going home for holidays. Middle class boys could also go to local grammar schools, which were day schools rather than boarding schools.

Some **working class** children were taught to read, write and do simple maths at small local schools that charged a small fee, or at Sunday school run by the church. The poorest children could go to **ragged schools**, set up from 1840 onwards. However, most working class children had no education at all and were expected to start working for wages as soon as possible.

In early Victorian times some children went to dame schools run by one woman. The painting probably makes this dame school look cleaner and less crowded than it really was.

This shows the monitorial system in action. Several monitors are being supervised by a teacher at the front of the class.

Education for all?

During the Victorian period, more and more workers needed to be able to read, write and do simple maths to do their jobs properly. At first the government left other groups to provide education, mostly church or charity organizations. Many schools used the 'monitorial' system. This system had large classes grouped by ability, taught by **monitors** chosen from the older children.

As the government made more rules about education it had to begin to provide and supervise that education. From 1833 it had given grants of money to some schools. In 1862 it set up a system for inspecting schools. In 1871 the government said local authorities had to provide schools where there were not enough church or charity-run schools, to give a school place to every child. From 1880 all children had to go to school between the ages of five and ten. However, schools still charged fees. By 1886 only about half the children who should have been in schools were actually going. In 1891 the government made education free and compulsory for all children between the ages of five and thirteen.

Exploring further – Learning about the world

Books that have survived tell us about what children learned in Victorian schools. Follow this path to read an extract from a Victorian textbook:

Contents > Written Sources > Transport and education

What were schools like in about 1900?

Children were put in large classes, sometimes over fifty children to a class. They sat at desks in rows facing the teacher and blackboard at the front of the class. They were taught as a class and learned a lot by reciting over and over. Some children were allowed to leave school at eleven years if they had reached the right 'Standard' or proved that their family needed their wages.

When children needed to write they began by writing on a piece of slate with chalk. The slate could be wiped and used over and over. Older children wrote on paper, using a pen with a steel nib that had to be dipped into a pot of ink every few words.

'Standards'

Children were taught to Standards, which were special levels of achievement tested yearly by government inspectors. They were expected to stay at school until they passed Standard Six. A school inspector wrote, in 1869:

It is possible to get the children through the reading, writing and mathematics exam without them really knowing how to read, write or do mathematics. A book is chosen at the beginning of the year for each Standard. All year the children read this book, over and over. When the inspector comes they can read a sentence or two from this book, but cannot read any other book easily.

Slates could be used in every subject and wiped clean after use.

This school was built in Victorian times. It is still used as a school now.

What did schools teach?

Schools taught children to read, write and do maths. They also taught history and geography. Some schools also taught science. Schools did not teach music or PE in the way that schools do now, although children sometimes did 'drill' in the classroom. Drill was a series of exercises that were done by the side of a desk.

One girl's memory of school in 1893:

I walked there with my brother. It was about two miles away. We had to be there at 9am and left at quarter to 4. We got an hour for lunch and had to take our lunch in tins, and it was put on the classroom stove to heat up. My cousin lived in town and her school let kids go home for lunch and gave hot dinners to those who stayed in school. Once we were at school I didn't see Ben until home time. We were in different classes and the boys' playground was separate from ours.

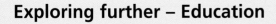

Exploring further – Education

To discover more about Victorian schools, follow this path:

Contents > Exploring > Everyday Life > Education

Click on the pictures on the left of the screen to find out what they show.

How did different Victorian children use their spare time?

Children used their spare time differently, depending on their social class. When they were not at work, poorer children tended to look after each other in large groups – playing on the streets or in the fields.

Middle class families often had a nursery or schoolroom for the children, but they were not expected to spend all their time there and shared some mealtimes with their parents. Most middle class families spent leisure time amusing themselves as a family by playing games, singing together or listening to one of the family reading aloud.

Upper class children had nurseries, bedrooms and schoolrooms in a separate part of the house to the adults. They often ate separately and they were brought up by nannies.

Daily games

Upper and middle class children usually had more time to play with toys than **working class** children, who often worked long hours. They also had more toys to play with. On the other hand, working class children tended to all play together, out of doors, and so had more children to play with.

These children in a town have made the lamppost into a type of swing.

 Boys and girls were given different sorts of toys. This set of 'dressing-up' dolls was a girl's toy.

Toys

Most children had a few toys like a ball or a doll. Girls got dolls and tea sets; boys got toy soldiers and marbles. Some toys, like board games or alphabet cubes were given to both boys and girls. Upper class children had beautiful expensive toys. Working class children had home-made toys.

Sundays

Sunday was a day when most children had spare time. However they could not play with their toys. They went to church and could read or play quietly with toys that had a religious connection –
like a Noah's ark.

Victorian rhymes reminded children that Sunday was a special day:

> I must not play on Sunday,
> Because it is a sin.
> Tomorrow will be Monday
> And then I can begin.

Exploring further – Digging deeper

The Digging Deeper section of the CD-ROM allows you to find out more about the topics that interest you. There is lots of information about the children in Victorian times. Follow this path:

Contents > Digging Deeper > Victorian Children
Click on the words in blue to explore further.

Christmas

Religion also provided fun days for children. The most important of these was Christmas. Many of our Christmas traditions began in Victorian times, including gifts under the tree, carol singing and Christmas cards.

Days out

Trains let Victorians travel further than ever before at a far lower cost. This, and the arrival of Bank Holidays and 'days off', meant that a new **working class** leisure activity sprang up – the cheap day **excursion**. Tour companies organized cheap train travel to special events. One of the first events visited in this way was the Great Exhibition of 1851.

Thomas Cook (1808–1892)

Thomas Cook was one of the first people to see how railway excursions could become popular. He organized his first excursion in 1841 from Leicester to Loughborough. It cost a shilling and included the rail trip, brass band music all the way and tea and buns in the park. Cook then organized trips to the Great Exhibition and seaside towns for the workers and far more expensive trips abroad, so the upper class could avoid Cook's 'excursioneers'!

The railways made seaside holidays popular for many more people.

Holidays

In Victorian times the idea of almost everyone having a yearly holiday began. As the Victorian period passed, laws came in to restrict working time. By the end of the period, most workers had Sundays and one other day off. They also did not have to work on Bank Holidays, introduced in 1871. Most employers allowed their workers to take a week's holiday (although they did not pay them during that time).

Workers did various things with their holidays. Some stayed at home. Others went to stay at the seaside for a week, taking cheap excursion trains and staying in cheap lodgings. Others, especially Londoners, went to work picking fruit and **hops** on farms in Kent. They had to live in tents in the fields, in very basic conditions. However, they earned enough money to cover the trip, and had a change of scene and lots of fresh air.

Summer holidays

A Manchester woman remembers her childhood in the 1890s:

Once a year, during **Wakes Week**, all the mills closed down. Each area had a different week, all through the summer. Most people went to Blackpool, though some went to Morecombe, even Rhyl. You went with your neighbours and were never lonely. You stayed in the same lodgings every year.

Exploring further – Holidays

Try searching for information about Victorian holidays, using the keyword Holidays. You can find out how to search the CD-ROM in the box on page 15.

How did life change for children living in Victorian Britain?

Life changed a lot less for upper class children between 1837 and 1901 than it did for **working class** children. They still did not need to work, and girls were still expected to marry and run a home.

New laws

The new laws brought in by the government meant that, as long as the laws were obeyed, working class children grew up in healthier homes with basic plumbing. They had education and started work later. When they did start work, they worked in better conditions for shorter hours.

All the same?

Different working class children had very different experiences. This was true even in the same town, let alone in different parts of the country.

New inventions

New inventions had changed the lives of many children, too. The railways meant their families could travel more, for work and leisure.

This photo shows passengers on a bus in 1890. Buses were a new form of transport and they were cheap enough for many of the poor to ride, rather than walk.

Two different views of farm work, from people interviewed at the end of the nineteenth century:

When I was a lad, I had to go to work on the farm every day from the age of six. The hours were long and the work was hard and all by hand. Now the work is done by machine and children are either at school or better employed for higher wages.

I started work in 1865, as a farm boy. My son started work as a farm boy last year, on the same farm. What he earns is maybe worth a bit more, but he's still doing the same job, in the same way and it's hard. But there's not other work for him, so he has to go.

In 1837 many children had terrible lives in **factories**. However, there were a few factory owners who looked after their workers, even then. In the same way, there were still factory owners breaking the rules in 1901. There were many places in the countryside where life went on in exactly the same way as it had in 1837.

What we can say for certain is that most people in 1901 had different ideas about children's education and working conditions.

Cities certainly had changed by 1900, when this photo was taken. Roads were paved and there were pavements and streetlights. Buses, trams and bicycles were new kinds of transport.

Exploring further – Pictures as evidence

Use the CD-ROM to find out more about changes in Victorian Britain. To see a bank of pictures of the time follow this path:

Contents > Pictures > Change and Influences
Click on one of the pictures to make it bigger. A caption will tell you what the picture shows.

How did life change in our locality during Victorian times?

Your **locality** almost certainly changed in Victorian times. If you live in a city there will be lots of changes; but even deep in the countryside schools and railways were built. A good step to find out about your locality in Victorian times is to walk around your area, looking at the buildings.

What evidence of Victorian times remains in our area?

Some Victorian buildings to look out for in your area are:

Public buildings, such as town halls and museums: rich Victorians wanted buildings to show their wealth and pride in their town.

Railway lines and stations: railways spread across the country. Many Victorian railway stations are still standing.

Schools: there were far more schools at the end of the Victorian period than there were at the beginning.

You can find out a lot about your area in Victorian times by looking at factories, houses, shops and churches that were built then.

This Victorian house in Reading was built in the 1890s.

Finding the Evidence

Libraries: go to the local history section. These have collections of photos, books, maps, newspapers, **trade** and **street directories**.

County Record Offices: these have the most information, including **census** material and many more maps and other written documents, as well as most of the things you would find in the public library. Many of them produce information packs about your local area.

Local museums: these often have Victorian collections ranging from clothes to farming equipment to reconstructions of rooms or shops.

Parish churches: these have records of births, christenings, marriages and burials. Churchyards often have many Victorian burials that provide information about how long people lived.

Private houses: some large houses are open to the public and have Victorian things on display. Some even have people living there for part of the time, acting as Victorians.

Using the evidence

Different kinds of evidence can show you different things. For example *Street directories* show how towns grew (as more and more streets are added). They also tell you the names of people who lived in the streets, so show you how families moved around. Sometimes families live in the same street for several generations, sometimes they move on quickly.

Trade directories tell you the shops and businesses in various parts of a town or city. You can see if the same sorts of businesses were in the same part of town (in earlier times, for instance, all the butchers would sell meat in a street called Butchers Row). If so, you might want to look at a map to work out why they want to be there – some businesses used a lot of water, for example, so needed to be close to the river.

Exploring further – Growth of towns and cities

During the Victorian period, many of our towns and cities got much bigger. Follow this path on the CD-ROM to see how some towns grew:

Contents > Written Sources > The growth of British towns
Your town may have grown during Victorian times.

The census – a closer look at one kind of evidence

Who lived here in 1841 and 1891?

Censuses have been taken every 10 years since 1841 to find out information about the population of the country. Census information is useful for showing how the population changed. It also tells you about the sizes of families and the work that people did. So you can notice new jobs, such as 'railway worker', which come with new inventions. There are many more schoolteachers in 1891 than in 1841 – the government expected children to go school and had provided schools for them to go to.

 This cartoon shows the problems census takers had, even if they were trying to be accurate.

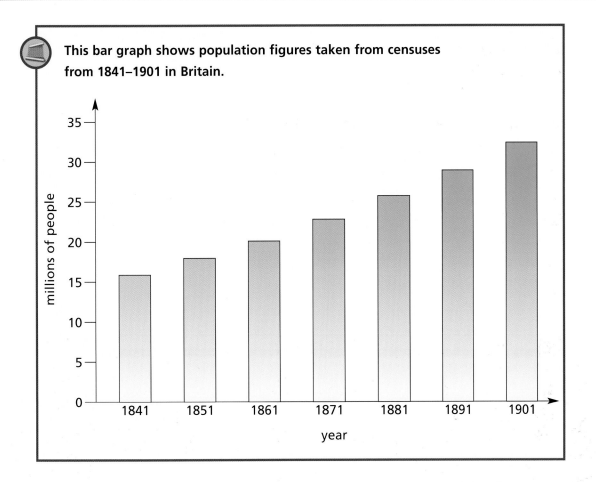

This bar graph shows population figures taken from censuses from 1841–1901 in Britain.

However, census information can sometimes look more accurate than it really is. For example, the census for England and Wales in 1801 was 8,892,536. In 1851 it was 17,927,609 and in 1891 it was 29,002,525. This looks very accurate indeed. But there were problems with census taking. Some census takers entered the wrong information by mistake and some made up information, to save work. Sometimes people did not tell census takers the truth. People who worked at night were not counted in the census (it was of people who were in the house on a particular night). This does not make the information useless. It was mostly right but it is better used to produce information like the chart shown here, than to give exact numbers.

Exploring further – The coming of the railways

The development of railways had a major effect in some areas. Follow this path to find more about the growth of railways in Victorian Britain:

Contents > Digging Deeper > Victorian Railways
Click on the words in blue to explore further.

Timeline

1819	Victoria born
1837	Victoria becomes queen, aged eighteen
1840	Victoria marries her cousin, Albert First ragged schools set up
1845-50	Potato famine in Ireland; many Irish people emigrate, especially to the USA
1851	First census to list occupations Great Exhibition
1861	Prince Albert dies
1863	First underground railway line opens in London
1867	Dr Barnardo opens Juvenile Mission in East End of London
1870	Dr Barnardo opens first home for boys
1871	First FA Cup competition for football
1877	Queen Victoria proclaimed 'Empress of India'
1880	Children must go to school aged 5–10; local authorities to employ 'truant officers' to make sure they do
1882	First electric power station in London
1891	Free education in state schools, for children aged 5–13
1897	Queen Victoria's Diamond Jubilee (Queen for 50 years)
1901	Victoria dies. Oldest son, Edward, becomes King Edward VII

Glossary

census   a count of all the people the country on a particular day

county record office   An office where records of all births, deaths, marriages and events of note are held for the county area

domestic service   to do household work such as cleaning and cooking in an upper-class house

excursions   trips or outings

factory   short for 'manufactory', a place where lots of workers and machines made large amounts of the same thing (for example, cloth)

hiring fairs   fairs held to match workers with employers

hops   a plant whose flowers are dried and used in beer brewing and medicines

industrialized   where heavy mechanized or factory industries, like mining and cloth-making, have been widely developed

locality   area or neighbourhood

manufactured   something made on a large scale using machinery

middle class   the middle of the Victorian class system, including anyone from a lawyer earning £500 a year to a small shopkeeper earning £100 a year

mission   a religious institution providing help or care for the poor or disadvantaged

monitors   one of the older school pupils who also teaches younger pupils

paupers   very poor people who have no way of feeding or supporting themselves

profit   money that is made from producing or selling something

ragged schools   a school set up to teach poor children

reign   the length of time a king or queen rules a country

scullery   a room near the kitchen, with a sink for washing up

street directories   lists of all the streets in a town or city, with the numbers of the houses and the names of the people living there

trade directories   books that list shops and tradespeople in each town or city

traps   wooden doors which were opened and closed to allow fresh air into mines

Wakes Week   The annual week's holiday given in summer to workers in factory towns

workhouses   places set up by the government where poor people with no money could go and be given a bed, food and work

working class   the bottom of the Victorian class system. A working class man could be anyone from a skilled mechanic earning £90 a year to a servant earning £10 a year.

Index